# The Mi'kmaq

## CHRISTINE WEBSTER

**Weigl**

CALGARY
www.weigl.com

Published by Weigl Educational Publishers Limited
6325 10 Street SE
Calgary, Alberta, Canada
T2H 2Z9

Website: www.weigl.com

Library and Archives Canada Cataloguing in Publication Data

Webster, Christine
        Mi'kmaq / Christine Webster.

(Canadian Aboriginal art and culture)
Includes index.
ISBN 978-1-55388-341-8 (bound)
ISBN 978-1-55388-342-5 (pbk.)

        1. Micmac Indians--Juvenile literature.  I. Title.  II. Series.
E99.M6W43 2007        j971.004'97343        C2007-902198-0

Printed in the United States of America
2 3 4 5 6 7 8 9 0  11 10 09

**Project Coordinator** Heather Kissock   **Design** Janine Vangool   **Validator** Craig Pierro, Wagmatcook Culture & Heritage Centre

**Photograph credits**
Every reasonable effort has been made to trace ownership and to obtain permission to reprint copyright material. The publishers would be pleased to have any errors or omissions brought to their attention so that they may be corrected in subsequent printings.

**Cover (top left):** History Collection, Nova Scotia Museum, Halifax; **Cover (top right):** © Canadian Museum of Civilization (III-F-248, D2004-22179); **Cover (main):** © Canadian Museum of Civilization (III-F-16 a,b, D2004-22215); © **Canadian Museum of Civilization:** pages 10 (III-F-108, D2004-23796), 11 (III-F-104, D2005-21165), 15 top (III-F-128, D2004-23175), 15 bottom (III-F-90, D2005-20177), 20 (III-F-213 a,b, D2004-22836), 24 (III-F-248, D2004-22179), 25 left (III-F-299, D2004-23240), 25 right (III-F-333, D2004-23229), 28 top (III-F-152, D2004-22912), 28 middle (III-F-129, D2004-22922), 28 bottom (III-F-216, D2004-22175), 29 (III-F-16 a,b, D2004-22215), and 30 (V-D-310, D2004-27600); **CP Images:** pages 1, 3, and 23; **Library and Archives Canada:** pages 6 (C-103533), 9 (C-000847), and 16 (C-028553); **History Collection, Nova Scotia Museum, Halifax:** pages 8, 17 left, 21, 22, and 26; **Courtesy of the Nova Scotia College of Art and Design (NSCAD):** page 27; **University of Newfoundland:** page 7.

We acknowledge the financial support of the Government of Canada through the Book Publishing Industry Development Program (BPIDP) for our publishing activities.

**Please note**

# CONTENTS

# The People

The Mi'kmaq are a group of **First Nations** peoples that live throughout eastern Canada. The term Mi'kmaq comes from the Aboriginal word *nikmak*. This means "my **kin** friends." There are other spellings of the word Mi'kmaq, including Micmac, Míqmaq, Míkmaq, and Mi'mkaq. Mi'kmaq is pronounced "mick-mack."

The Mi'kmaq have lived in eastern Canada for more than 10,000 years. In the past, they were hunter-gatherers. During the winter, they hunted along the rivers, where they found bear, deer, moose, caribou, and beaver. In the summer, they moved toward the ocean coast. Here, they fished, caught seabirds, and speared porpoises. They also gathered berries and other plants to use as food and medicine.

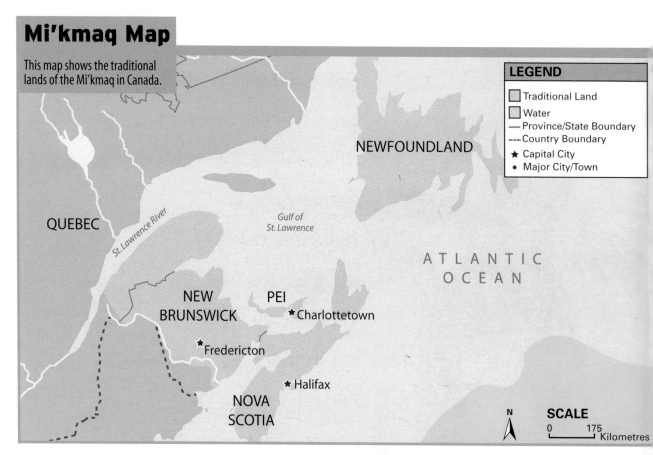

## Mi'kmaq Map

This map shows the traditional lands of the Mi'kmaq in Canada.

NEWFOUNDLAND

**LEGEND**
- ☐ Traditional Land
- ☐ Water
- — Province/State Boundary
- --- Country Boundary
- ★ Capital City
- ● Major City/Town

QUEBEC

St. Lawrence River

Gulf of St. Lawrence

ATLANTIC OCEAN

NEW BRUNSWICK

PEI
★ Charlottetown

★ Fredericton

★ Halifax

NOVA SCOTIA

N

SCALE
0    175
└────┘ Kilometres

The Mi'kmaq settled into seven territories, or districts. These areas stretched across Prince Edward Island, Nova Scotia, New Brunswick, Newfoundland, and Quebec. In the 1860s, another district was added. It was Taqamkuk, which is located in southern Newfoundland.

Today, there are about 20,000 Mi'kmaq living in Canada. About one-third of this population can read, write, and speak the Mi'kmaq language.

Today, many Mi'kmaq live and work in cities. Others live on **reserves**. Here, they continue their ancestors' traditions. While many Mi'kmaq make a living as part of the fishing industry, they have now expanded into other areas as well, including tourism and logging.

**The lobster fishing industry provides jobs for many Mi'kmaq today.**

# Mi'kmaq Homes

The Mik'maq lived in homes called wigwams. A wigwam was shaped like a cone or dome. Its frame was built using poles made out of spruce. Once the frame was ready, it was covered with bark.

The word "wigwam" comes from the Mi'kmaq word *wikuom*. Wikuom means "dwelling." Wigwams were designed to be built quickly and moved easily. A wigwam took about one day to build. It was easily taken apart. The materials could be moved to different locations and used again. A wigwam was mostly built by women. They worked together to build one. Usually, one woman oversaw the project.

The floor of the wigwam was covered with twigs, woven mats, and animal furs for sleeping and sitting.

To build a wigwam, women needed poles to make the frame. Branches from spruce trees provided the five to ten poles needed. One end of each pole was placed in the ground. The other end was then bent over and tied together with ropes of spruce root. This formed the dome shape. A hoop made from a bent sapling kept the poles from collapsing. It was placed near the top, inside the frame.

Large wigwams could house as many as 15 people.

Large sheets of birchbark were sewn to the frame to provide a cover. Birchbark was a good resource as it is waterproof. Spruce root was used to sew the sheets into place. The sheets were punched with holes using a bone **awl**. The birchbark was kept warm and wet during this process. This stopped it from tearing as it was sewn. Starting at the bottom, the pieces were sewn into place. They were overlapped like shingles are on today's houses. This kept wind, rain, and cold weather out.

A fire pit was kept in the middle of the wigwam. The fire pit kept the home warm and gave the Mi'kmaq heat, light, and a place to cook. The top of the wigwam was left open to allow smoke from the fire pit to escape. Extra poles were placed on the outside. This held the wigwam firmly in place to protect it from high winds. A piece of thick animal hide hung over the entrance as a door.

# Mi'kmaq Communities

The Mi'kmaq lived in **harmony** with each other. Each community had a local chief. The chief, together with a council of **elders**, was responsible for the villages within the community.

Each community belonged to a larger district. Each district also had a chief, who was called the Saqamaw. The Saqamaw was the most respected person in the district. He oversaw all the local chiefs.

The Saqamaw had many responsibilities. He assigned hunting grounds among the communities, solved problems within his district, and led his people into battle if necessary. He also represented his district to other districts. The Saqamaw was responsible for forming **alliances** with other districts, negotiating hunting and fishing areas for his district, and addressing any conflicts that his district may have with another district.

Chiefs were important within the Mi'kmaq community, as well as the provinces in which they lived. In the 1800s, Chief John Noel was responsible for the Mi'kmaqs in Halifax and its surrounding area. During his time as chief, he was presented with medals by the king of England and the Pope.

The Mi'kmaq had their own rules and ways of living. They worked, lived, and played as a group. The community resolved problems as a group. Each community was made up of 50 to 500 members. They travelled throughout eastern Canada according to the seasons. Men were responsible for protecting the community. They also did the hunting and fishing. Women gathered plants for cooking and took care of the camps and children. Sometimes, when men were hunting, the women took over their roles. They fished to support their families until the men returned.

Sometimes, individual Mi'kmaq groups would come together to form larger groups of up to 300 people. This normally happened when food sources, such as deer or fish, were abundant in the area.

# THE GRAND COUNCIL

The Mi'kmaq had their own form of government. It was called the Mi'kmaq Grand Council. The Grand Council was a system of government that allowed all district chiefs to meet. The most important decisions were made within the council. The council would elect one main chief. He was called the Grand Saqamaw. The Grand Saqamaw was the spokesperson of the Mi'kmaq. His responsibilities included relations with other Aboriginal groups. The Grand Saqamaw also met with Europeans and formed agreements with them. The first series of **treaties** came in 1725, when the Grand Council signed an agreement with the British. This treaty assured the British that the Mi'kmaq would be loyal to them. In exchange, the Mi'kmaq could continue to hunt and fish in peace.

The Grand Council still meets today. All Mi'kmaq reserves are governed by it.

# Mi'kmaq Clothing

Everything the Mi'kmaq wore was created by their own hands. They used resources from the land around them. Most Mi'kmaq clothing was made from animal skins. This included deer and caribou. The skins were stretched and tanned. This process produced beautiful leather and furs. Bone awls were used as needles to sew pieces together. **Sinew** was picked into fine strands for thread.

Men wore leggings made from caribou or moose skins. The skins were tied at the hip to a belt. Men also wore breechcloths, which were cloths that hung from the waist. In colder weather, fur robes were worn like a blanket over the shoulders. Women also wore leggings and robes. The robes were wrapped around the body under the arms and were tied at the waist with a belt. Children dressed similar to adults. Babies were wrapped in soft furs. Fox, swan, and goose down kept them warm.

Women often wore a pointed hat instead of a headdress.

By the 19th century, materials were being traded between the Mi'kmaq and the Europeans. Mi'kmaq clothing reflected this. Robes made from skins were replaced with woollen ones. Jackets, skirts, and caps were introduced. Men's robes looked similar to military uniforms.

The Mi'kmaq loved to decorate their clothing with **geometric** designs. Red and yellow **ochre** was used for colour. White shells were ground up to make a fine powder. These ingredients were mixed with bird egg yolks or animal fat to make paint. The paint was used to colour clothing. Other dyes came from roots, bark, leaves, and flowers. These dyes could be used to paint porcupine quills. The coloured quills were placed in a unique pattern on the clothing.

Animal teeth, claws, and bones were also sewn onto clothing as ornaments. Feathers were a popular decoration, too. Men would sometimes wear bird wings on the sides of their head. When the Europeans arrived in North America, many new ornaments, such as ribbons and beads, were introduced through trading. Mi'kmaq women used the beads and ribbons to make beautiful designs.

Deer and caribou were still used to make clothing after the Europeans arrived. Clothes became more European in appearance, however.

# Mi'kmaq Food

The Mi'kmaq obtained their food mostly from the forests and the sea. They ate salmon, sturgeon, whale, walrus, seal, squid, eel, and lobster. They also caught game. This included moose, caribou, beaver, porcupine, and small animals, such as squirrels. The meat from the game and fish was dried and smoked. This preserved it for the winter months. In the summer, berries, roots, and edible plants were gathered.

The Mi'kmaq planned their lives around the **migration** cycles of the animals. Beginning in January, the Mi'kmaq hunted seals along the coast. From February to mid-March, they moved inland to hunt moose, caribou, beaver, and bear. At the end of March, they returned to the coast to catch smelt, a type of fish. In April, herring was also available. Throughout spring, the Mi'kmaq would rely on sea birds and salmon as well. From May to September, they fished and gathered shellfish. Then, they moved to large rivers where they would catch eel. By October, the Mi'kmaq moved back inland to hunt large game. In December, when the waters were frozen, cod was taken from underneath the ice.

The Mi'kmaq hunted walrus mainly off the southern coast of Newfoundland and in the Gulf of St. Lawrence.

## Luskikan (Mi'kmaq Bread)

Ingredients

1.2 litres flour

20 millilitres baking powder

4 millilitres salt

12 millilitres butter

60 millilitres water

Equipment

**Bowl**

**Spoon**

**Bread pan**

**Knife**

1. Put the flour, baking powder, butter, and salt into the bowl.

2. Add water, and mix into a soft dough.

3. Pat the dough into the bread pan.

4. Cut the dough in squares using a knife that is covered in flour.

5. Bake for about 45 minutes at 150 degrees Celsius.

# Tools, Weapons, and Defence

Tools were essential to everyday life. The Mi'kmaq needed tools to cut wood, hunt animals, and protect themselves. To make tools and weapons, the Mi'kmaq used many items from the natural world. These included animal bones, teeth, claws, fur, feathers, leather, quills, shells, clay, stones, and wood.

Blades were made by chipping at stones to give them sharp edges. The stone was then tied to a stick of wood to make an axe or adze. Beaver teeth were used for carving. Bones were used to make sewing needles and also weapons.

The Mi'kmaq caught fish using weirs. A weir is a type of trap. To make a weir, the Mi'kmaq placed stakes firmly into a stream bed. Then, branches were woven between the stakes to block the river. The fish were forced to swim into the weir. Once trapped by the weir, the fish could be speared in large numbers.

The Mi'kmaq used birchbark to make canoes because it is waterproof. Canoes were useful tools for travel.

# HUNTING AND TRAVELLING

The Mi'kmaq used different weapons for hunting and fishing. They used bows and arrows and spears to hunt large game animals. A special type of stone called chalcedony was used to make the points on these weapons. This stone easily flakes away to form a razor-sharp edge. Bone points were often used as spears to harpoon fish or seals.

Bows and arrows were used to hunt animals such as moose, deer, and caribou.

The Mi'kmaq had a special technique they used to lure moose to them. They made a horn out of birchbark. When they blew into the horn, a sound similar to a moose call came out. A moose would be attracted to the call and would come toward the Mi'kmaq. This made the moose hunt easier for the hunters.

Another important tool the Mi'kmaq made were snowshoes. Snowshoes allowed the Mi'kmaq to easily walk over the deep snow. This gave the them an advantage while hunting. Heavy animals were slowed down by deep snow. They could not run as fast as the hunters.

# Mi'kmaq Religion

The Mi'kmaq believed that everything in the world was alive and deserved respect. This included humans, animals, rocks, and dirt. To honour this belief, the Mi'kmaq wasted nothing. They only took what they needed from nature. They thanked the Creator for what they took. The Mi'kmaq believed the Creator made everything in the world. Nothing was taken without praying for his guidance. The Mi'kmaq believed the Creator was good and kind.

The Mi'kmaq believed that people went to a special place when they died. It was called the Land of Souls. Here, the dead were welcomed by their ancestors and the Creator.

Healers, such as Jerry Lonecloud, received guidance from the spirit world when treating illnesses.

The Mi'kmaq believed in evil spirits. Evil spirits caused bad things, such as diseases and hunger, to happen. Like many Aboriginal groups, the Mi'kmaq had **shamans** in their communities. The shamans cured illness and removed evil spirits.

In the early 1600s, French missionaries met with the Mi'kmaq and began to teach them about **Christianity**. Eventually, many Mi'kmaq adopted Christian beliefs.

The Mi'kmaq consider feathers to be **sacred**. The Eagle is believed to be the only creature to touch the face of the Creator. Receiving an eagle feather is a great honour. Only someone who is unselfish in helping the community will receive one.

The Mi'kmaq's first experiences with Christianity came from contact with French Jesuit missionaries. The Jesuits were one of the first religious orders to come to what is now Canada.

# Ceremonies and Celebrations

L ike all societies, the Mi'kmaq held ceremonies and celebrations. One ancient ceremony took place in a sweat lodge. A sweat lodge was dome shaped like a wigwam. It was usually made from willow bushes. In the center was a firepit. The door always faced east.

The sweat lodge was a place of **spiritual** communication. It was where the Mi'kmaq went to pray and purify the mind and body. As soon as people entered the lodge, praying would begin.

**The Mi'kmaq pray to the Creator to give thanks and to ask for things.**

Usually, about four to twelve people took part in a sweat lodge ceremony. Once inside the lodge, they would sit around the fire pit and pray. The dugout contained preheated rocks that created the heat and steam needed for the ceremony. There were set times, called "rounds," when the door could be opened. This relieved others briefly from the heat. The purpose of the ceremony, however, was to sweat. It was believed that this removed impurities from the body. When the ceremony ended, the participants would emerge from the sweat lodge feeling spiritually and physically cleansed.

Each January, the Mi'kmaq held a feast. This occurred after the first new moon. This feast was called the Mid Winter Feast, or *Wi'kapaltimk Aqtapuk*. The feast marked the end of the year. It was also a time to celebrate the new year ahead. During the feast, the Mi'kmaq thanked the Creator. They gave thanks for their blessings, health, and food. They celebrated with stories, speeches, dances, and food.

**The entrance to a Mi'kmaq sweat lodge always faces east. The East symbolizes light, energy, and the sunrise.**

# Music and Dance

Chanting and drumming are an important part of Mi'kmaq spirituality. The Mi'kmaq use drums in ceremonies, and for dancing and singing. The drum represents the centre of life.

Before drumming begins, the drums are blessed. There are four parts to the blessing. First, the drums are blessed to the East, and thanks are given to the Eagle for giving guidance to the Mi'kmaq people. They are then blessed to the South, and thanks are given to the grandmothers and mothers for giving life to children. The third blessing is directed to the West and the spirit world. The final blessing is given to the North and the White Bear. The White Bear gives the Mi'kmaq strength and courage when facing life's challenges.

Drums often accompany chants, or songs. One of the best-known Mi'kmaq chants is the Honour Song. It blends human and animal sounds to tell the story of how the Eagle came to help the Mi'kmaq.

The Mi'kmaq believe that the drumbeat represents the heartbeat of Mother Earth.

Dancing is a way for the Mi'kmaq to tell stories and entertain others. In the past, a common event was the re-enactment of a successful hunt. During a dangerous part of the story, the drum would beat fiercely. The dancer might pretend to be the hunter or the animal. To add more noise to their dance, the Mi'kmaq tied bones or teeth to a stick and shook them.

Many Mi'kmaq dances are sacred. The Sun Dance is performed as a sacrifice to help people who are sick. The dancers go without water for several days, so the dance requires a great deal of training. When dancing, the performers pay tribute to the Sun, Earth, and the four directions—north, south, east, and west.

Prayer is an important part of Mi'kmaq dancing. Many dances are performed in honour of spirits or ancestors.

# Language and Storytelling

The Mi'kmaq language comes from the **Algonquian** language family. It is a very rich and descriptive language. The Mi'kmaq language has 11 consonants. These are p, t, k, q, j, s, l, m, n, w, and y. It also has five vowels, a, e, i, o, and u. Most Mi'kmaq words are verbs, meaning that they relate to the actions of people and animals.

The Mi'kmaq wrote messages called hieroglyphics, which were scratched onto birchbark or animal hides. A hieroglyphic is a picture that tells a story. The reader can look at the picture and understand what the writer is saying. A man named Silas T. Rand studied the Mi'kmaq language. He used the English alphabet to sound out the language. This helped him create an English form of the Mi'kmaq language. He then translated parts of the Bible into Mi'kmaq.

Silas T. Rand could speak many languages besides English and Mi'kmaq. He knew two other First Nations languages and several European languages.

Since the 1970s, there has been a decline in Mi'kmaq speakers. The Mi'kmaq are taking steps to keep the language alive. They have brought the language back into their schools. Today, the Mi'kmaq language is spoken by about 7,500 people. Different **dialects** are spoken in the many areas where the Mi'kmaq live.

The Mi'kmaq liked to entertain each other through storytelling. They used storytelling as a way to share information. The art of storytelling has been passed down for generations. The beating of the drum signalled the start of a storytelling session. Some stories were hours long. Power is a main theme in all Mi'kmaq stories. Stories explore how power is used, lost, and gained.

Mi'kmaq children are introduced to traditional languages and music at an early age.

# Mi'kmaq Art

The Mi'kmaq were creative craftspeople. Many of the items they made for everyday use are now considered art. Everything from their woven baskets and beaded clothing to their porcupine-quilled boxes was uniquely crafted.

The change from everyday use to works of art started soon after the Mi'kmaq made contact with Europeans. By the 1600s, Mi'kmaq women were making crafts to trade with Europeans. The Mi'kmaq began by trading woven baskets. Baskets were made from maple, poplar, and ash trees. For years, the baskets were traded for European goods. By the 19th century, the Mi'kmaq were travelling to cities and towns to sell their baskets at markets. This created an **economy** for the Mi'kmaq.

Basketry was an important part of Mi'kmaq daily life. Everyone in the family had a job to do when a basket was being made. These jobs included weaving the basket and selecting the tree to be used.

# DOLL-MAKING

The Mi'kmaq were well-known for their porcupine quillwork. Each quill was dipped into brightly coloured paints. The coloured quills were used to make a **mosaic**. They were carefully placed into holes in wet bark as ornaments. The beautifully decorated birchbark was used for other things. Sometimes, it was used for seat covers. Other times, it was used for decoration on the top of a wooden box.

Today, only a few Mi'kmaq continue the quillwork tradition. When glass beads were introduced by Europeans, the Mi'kmaq women began making beaded tea-cozies, purses, and vests with the beautiful beads instead. Many of these original arts have survived. They remain in museums around Canada.

Dolls played an important role in Mi'kmaq society. They were often miniature forms of the Mi'kmaq themselves and were dressed in the traditional garments of both men and women. Other items from Mi'kmaq life, such as canoes, were made in miniature as well. The dolls were used in a variety of ways. Sometimes, they were toys for children. Other dolls were made to represent characters from Mi'kmaq stories. They were used as tools to pass the story to younger generations.

Toys were one way that Mi'kmaq children were introduced to their heritage.

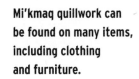

Mi'kmaq quillwork can be found on many items, including clothing and furniture.

# Petroglyphs

Early Mi'kmaq used drawings as a way to communicate with others. Sometimes, these drawings were carved onto rocks. These rock pictures are called petroglyphs. To make a petroglyph, the Mi'kmaq used stone or metal tools to scratch, cut, or peck lines into smooth rock surfaces. The images they drew were of people and animals. They also showed the Sun and stars. Sometimes, the petroglyphs told a story about hunting or fishing.

Petroglyphs are a recorded history of Mi'kmaq life. They show how early Mi'kmaq saw their life around them. Some signs on a petroglyph have specific meanings. A triangle represents life-giving energy. Circles represent the Sun. Some Mi'kmaq petroglyphs are believed to be more than 2,000 years old. Today, Mi'kmaq petroglyphs can be found along the rocky shores of Canada's eastern provinces.

The Mi'kmaq used petroglyphs to communicate about events such as wars and the arrival of the Europeans.

## Alan Syliboy

Alan Syliboy is a traditional Mi'kmaq artist. He lives on the Millbrook First Nation Reserve, which is located in Truro, Nova Scotia. Alan enjoyed drawing from an early age. He studied with a **Maliseet** artist. Her name was Shirley Bear. Shirley was Alan's spiritual guide as well as his art teacher. When Alan was older, he went to college. He attended the Nova Scotia College of Art and Design.

Alan found his inspiration from ancient Mi'kmaq petroglyphs. He used the petroglyph symbols of his ancestors in his paintings.

Alan wanted to show respect for his heritage through his art. He also wanted to create an art form that appealed to the public and to his people. He used the traditional designs of the Mi'kmaq petroglyphs to create original prints on T-shirts.  He sold these T-shirts door-to-door on his reserve and, later, on reserves throughout the Atlantic provinces.

Founded in 1887, the Nova Scotia College of Art and Design is one of North America's first art schools.

Today, Allan creates other forms of art as well. Allan makes prints, cards, sculpture, and pottery. Most of his work relates to family, struggles, and strength.

Alan's art can be found all across North America in both private and public collections. This includes the National Indian Art Collection of the Department of Indian and Northern Affairs.

In 1999, Alan expanded his art expertise further by designing a coin for the Royal Canadian Mint. It was called the Butterfly Gold Coin.

Today, Alan sits on the Board of Governors for the Nova Scotia College of Art and Design. He lives on the Millbrook First Nation Reserve with his three children.

# Studying the Past

Archaeologists study ancient peoples. The **artifacts** they find help them to determine how people, including the Mi'kmaq, lived in the past. Petroglyphs are just one of the artifacts that have helped archaeologists learn about early Mi'kmaq. Fragments of pottery archaeologists have found show that the Mi'kmaq used pots for cooking and storage. These pots were made from clay mixed with crushed rocks or shells. They were shaped with a stone or wood. Sometimes, designs were pressed into the pots. Earlier pots were very thin, but well made. Over time, the pots became thicker. These thick pots broke easily.

Archaeologists have discovered large deposits of seashells in parts of eastern Canada where the Mi'kmaq were known to live. Using this information, they believe that shellfish was a huge part of the Mi'kmaq diet. Along with these findings, archaeologists have found tools, arrows, and knives. These indicate how the Mi'kmaq hunted and travelled.

Items such as chisels, dishes, and spears can help archaeologists form theories about Mi'kmaq life in the past.

# TIMELINE

## 10,000 years ago
Ancestors of today's Mi'kmaq peoples' live in what is now eastern Canada.

## Pre-European Contact
The Mi'kmaq hunt moose and caribou, gather berries, and catch fish and whale for survival. They build settlements along riverbanks, lakes, and the ocean coast.

## AD 1497
Explorer John Cabot arrives on the eastern coast of what is now Canada.

## 1534
The first trade between Mi'kmaq and Europeans is recorded.

## 1606
Marc Lescarbot, a historian, provides the earliest detailed records of Mi'kmaq life.

## 1725
The Mi'kmaq and Maliseet sign a treaty with the British. It was the first of several peace treaties between the British and Mi'kmaq.

## 1779
The final treaty between the British and the Mi'kmaq is signed.

## 1801
The government of Nova Scotia sets aside 10 reserves for the Mi'kmaq.

## 1868
The Indian Act is created. This gives limited control to the First Nations peoples.

## 1983
Mi'kmaq petroglyphs are found in Bedford, Nova Scotia.

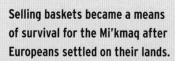

**Selling baskets became a means of survival for the Mi'kmaq after Europeans settled on their lands.**

# Porcupine-Quill Bracelet

The Mi'kmaq used porcupine quills to make beautiful embroidery patterns as well as jewellery. Bracelets were one type of jewellery they made from the quills. You can make a bracelet similar to those of the Mi'kmaq by following the instructions below.

## Materials

A combination of long, narrow beads and short, round beads

String, coloured wool, or leather

Scissors

A pencil

1. Cut a piece of string, wool, or leather so that it is about 50 centimetres long.

2. Thread both ends of the string through a single round bead. This will form a loop at one end.

3. Push a pencil through the loop to keep the string from being pulled all the way through the bead. There should now be two strands of string falling from the bead. These two strands will form the two strands of your bracelet.

4. Thread a long, narrow bead onto each cord.

5. Thread three round beads onto each cord.

6. Continue this pattern until the bracelet is long enough to fit around your wrist. Finish by threading both cords together through two round beads.

7. Take the pencil out of the loop.

8. Thread one cord through the loop.

9. Tie the two cords together with a double knot. Trim the ends with scissors.

10. Your bracelet is now complete. Slip it onto your wrist to wear it.

# Further Reading

To learn more about Canada's Mi'kmaq, read Robert Leavitt's *Mi'kmaq of the East Coast* (Fitzhenry and Whiteside, 2000).

*Red Earth: Tales of the Micmacs* by Marion Robertson (Nimbus Publishing, 2006) features many traditional legends of the Mi'kmaq.

# Websites

To learn more about Mi'kmaq heritage, visit **www.heritage.nf.ca/ aboriginal/micmac_culture.html**.

Aspects of Mi'kmaq history, daily life, and culture are featured at **www.collectionscanada.ca/ settlement/kids/021013-2091-e.html**

Take a look at some of Alan Syliboy's art at **www.redcrane.ca**.

# GLOSSARY

# INDEX

**Algonquian:** a family of languages spoken by First Nations peoples living mainly in central and eastern North America

**alliances:** unions formed by agreement

**archaeologists:** scientists who study objects from the past to learn about people who lived long ago

**artifacts:** items, such as tools, made by a human

**awl:** a pointed tool for making holes in wood or leather

**Christianity:** a religion based on the teachings of Jesus Christ

**dialects:** variations on a language that is spoken in a certain place

**economy:** a system of managing the production, distribution, and consumption of goods

**elders:** the older and more influential members of a community

**First Nations:** members of Canada's Aboriginal community who are not Inuit or Métis

**geometric:** characterized by straight lines, circles, triangles, and other shapes

**harmony:** to live in peace

**kin:** family or relatives

**Maliseet:** a First Nations group found in New Brunswick and Maine

**migration:** the movement from one place to another with the change in seasons

**mosaic:** a design made of small pieces of stone, glass, wood, or other items of different colours set together or inlaid

**ochre:** a type of earth mixed with iron, ranging in colour from yellow to red

**reserves:** land set aside by the government for First Nations peoples

**sacred:** worthy of religious worship

**shamans:** religious people who were believed to have special powers

**sinew:** tendons from animals

**spiritual:** sacred or religious

**treaties:** agreements between nations

*THE OFFICIAL*

# National Hockey League
# STANLEY CUP
## Centennial Book

THE OFFICIAL

# National Hockey League
# STANLEY CUP
## Centennial Book

E D I T E D   B Y   D A N   D I A M O N D

TORMONT

**Canadian Cataloguing in Publication Data (Canada)**

Main entry under title:
The Official National Hockey League Stanley Cup centennial book

2nd Canadian ed.
Includes index.

ISBN 2-89429-325-9

1. Stanley Cup (Hockey) – History.   2. National Hockey League – History.
I. Diamond, Dan.

BV847.7.044 1993          796.962'648          C93-096138-2


Editor: Dan Diamond
Photo Editor: Ralph Dinger
Sidebars and Captions: James Duplacey
Additional Research: Ron Boileau (PCHA/WCHL/WHL), Al Kowalenko
Main Text: Bob Hesketh, Jack Sullivan, James Duplacey, Dan Diamond
Index : Janet Goodfellow
Coordinating Editor: Pat Kennedy for McClelland & Stewart
Design: Kong Njo


Printed and bound in the United States of America.

Published in 1993 by
Tormont Publications Inc.
338 Saint Antoine St. East
Montreal, Quebec, Canada
H2Y 1A3
Tel. (514) 954-1441  Fax (514) 954-1443

*For everyone whose dreams
are inscribed on the Cup*

# Contents

# A Message from the President

For athletes, all efforts focus on becoming a champion. For the men who skate in the National Hockey League, there is no greater accomplishment than winning the Stanley Cup, which, for one hundred years, has stood at the pinnacle of hockey excellence. Nothing in professional sports matches the feeling of holding the trophy aloft as a member of a Cup-winning team.

In fact, in the century since its first presentation, the Stanley Cup has become the most recognizable trophy in all of sports – a clear and immediate symbol of accomplishment that combines the past and the present. Look inside the bowl and you'll find the names of the 1907 Cup-champion Kenora Thistles. Or see Lester Patrick's name inscribed as part of the Cup-winning Montreal Wanderers in 1906 – and then read his grandson Craig's name inscribed twice as the general manager of the Cup-winning Pittsburgh Penguins of 1991 and 1992.

This is the magic of the Stanley Cup, the ability to bring together the game's great names and golden eras. The winners literally hold history in their hands.

I am honored to open this fine book, and join with you in celebrating the centennial of the Stanley Cup.

Gil Stein,
*President,*
*National Hockey League*